From GRIEF To GLORY

Testimony and poetry of Tim Byrd

TIM BYRD

Copyright © 2017 by Tim Byrd

From Grief To Glory
Testimony and poetry of Tim Byrd
by Tim Byrd

Printed in the United States of America.

ISBN 9781498476577

All rights reserved solely by the author. The author guarantees all contents are original and do not infringe upon the legal rights of any other person or work. No part of this book may be reproduced in any form without the permission of the author. The views expressed in this book are not necessarily those of the publisher.

Unless otherwise indicated, Scripture quotations taken from the King James Version (KJV) – *public domain*.

www.xulonpress.com

INTRODUCTION:

My name is Tim Byrd, I want to **THANK YOU!!** For your interest in this book which contains my testimony and poems I have written up to this point of my life.

My testimony is one that many people share; I lived a life of alcohol and drug addiction, criminal activity, violence, and all the pleasures of this world Satan has to offer; but **Praise God!!** I was delivered from these strongholds of Satan through my lord and savior **Jesus Christ!**

The very fact that you're reading my words is a miracle of it's own; I'm lucky to be alive but on top of that I was kicked out of high school in the tenth grade and obtained my G.E.D, so I'm certainly not educated enough to write this book, but the ***Doors Jesus!! Can Open No Man Can Close,*** and I'm only one example of how ***"God"*** can use the foolish things of this world to confound the wise. ***1Cor. 1:27-But God has chosen the foolish things of the world to confound the wise; and God hath chosen the weak things of the world to confound the things which are mighty.***

So I just want to **Encourage YOU!** to chase your dreams, and allow ***"God"*** to prepare your path.

As long as you **Place God First** in your life; you have succeeded already! And remember; ***If I Can Do It! You Can Do It!!***

Matt.6:33- But seek ye first the kingdom of God and his righteousness; and all these things shall be added unto you.

About my poems: As I had previously mentioned; I am not an educated man. My **Poetry** is a **Gift** of words that ***"GOD"*** has chosen to give me. In my old life, I was a violent man who thought of people who wrote poetry as a **Bunch of Sissy's** so it just goes to prove that ***"God"*** has a sense of humor!

By my old standard my **Gift Of Poetry** makes me a **Sissy!**

Introduction

I started writing my poetry while I was locked up in the Perry county, Ms *Jail* awaiting trial on ***Drug Charges***

I sat down one day and began to write what ***"GOD"*** had put on my heart; once the words started flowing from my heart through my pen, it was as if someone else was doing the writing; I could not believe the words I was putting on paper, twenty four hours later I had written my first four poems. When I was done, I began to read my poems to the other ***Inmates*** and I couldn't believe the response I got? Most of the ***Hardened Criminals*** had tears in their eyes.

From that day forward, the men would ask me to write poems for their wives, mothers, and children, and through my poems I was able to ***minister*** to the ***other inmates*** I was locked up with. I truly ***"Hope You Enjoy"*** this series of poems.

DEDICATION:

First and foremost I want to dedicate this book to my **Lord And Savior Jesus Christ!!** without him **Nothing Would Be Possible** Never in a million years would I have thought **Jesus!!** could use someone like me? I also want to dedicate this book to my **Friend** my **Brother in Christ** and my **Ministry Partner** Brother **Raju Amruthapudi** and his lovely wife **Leelavathi.** Me and brother **Raj** are the founding members of **Continuing Strength international ministries** bro.**Raj** is a dedicated servant to our Lord **Jesus!!** and the ministry. **90 percent** of the proceeds from this book will go to the task of spreading **"God's Word"** in the country of **India** and the other **10 percent** will stay here in America to provide basic ministry needs.**Thank You!!** For your prayers and support in helping me fulfill the calling *"**God**"* has placed on my life please continue to pray for this small ministry.

Special thanx: Bro. Rory Dill:

Bro. Rory was one of the 12 step teachers and mentors at the mission. Thank you Bro. Rory for your prayers and taking my countless phone calls to answer my questions and give me information while I was researching the scriptures to write this book. I couldn't have done it without you. I hope one day to have your wisdom, and knowledge of God's word.

I love you Bro.Rory. Thank you!!

Special thanx: Bro. Harley Mercier.

I met Harley while I was at the mission at the cross; Harley is a mentor at the mission and shows up every day at 6:00 a.m for the morning devotion. Harley is also a youth minister at Moss first church of God.

And is also a veteran of our American military. Thank you for your service to our great country and thank you for your dedication to the ministry of our Lord Jesus. You have made a difference in my life and many other lives through your unselfish devotion as a mentor and friend. I also want to say thank you for editing this book. True to your kind and generous nature you took time out of your busy schedule to help me accomplish this goal and I am truely thankfull. I love you brother; Thank you!!

Hello, my name is; Timothy Mack Byrd. I was born at the old charity hospital in Laurel, ms. January 7th,1973. which makes me 43 years old. I am the oldest of three boys. born to my parents; Mack and Patricia Byrd.

My younger brother Matthew; was born may 1st,1974. My youngest brother Sam, was born January 14th,1977. My father was born; February 12th, 1950. With an inherited eye disease; which caused the nerves from his eyeballs to his brain to deteriorate over the course of his life. He was deemed legally blind at the age of 22. By the time he passed away in 2011; he was pretty much completely blind. I mention my dad's blindness; because his blindness was a big influence in how I grew up. By the time I was big enough to do anything, I was my Daddy's eyes; and his helper in everything. He taught me how to drive in the hay fields of Jones and Covington county when I was 5 years old. My first job was driving the ole hay truck for daddy, while he loaded the hay onto the truck. So believe me when I tell you there was some interesting moments that took place on those hot summer days in the hay fields. One of those moments that begs to be mentioned, is the first day I learned to drive a stick, I must have been around the age of ten.

I remember daddy putting me in his lap; and showing me how to go through the gears. The plan in the hayfield was to only use first gear; which meant all I had to do was come off the clutch, and let the truck putt-putt along the row of hay, and daddy would load the bail of hay as I came to it.I must admit, that sounds like a good plan. By all rights, it was a good plan. The moment of truth comes. I get behind the steering wheel ready to drive. But as it turned out I came off the clutch to fast and the truck began to buck like a mad bull out across the hay field. Every time the truck would buck my foot would hit the accelerator. I ended up on and off the accelerator out across the hay field. Daddy was finally able to chase me and the truck down; before I caused any real damage.

After a few more lessons from a very patient father. I was able to navigate the truck well enough that we managed to haul some hay. This is just one of many exciting events that took place with my daddy as a kid. Daddy was a very good man, with a great sense of humor. He just loved to have a good laugh! He taught me a lot of life's lessons out in the hay field or under the hood of an old Chevy. The thing I will never forget about daddy is the way he faced death. He was diagnosed with leukemia at the beginning of 2011. and in the month of April he was admitted to the university medical center in Jackson,ms. to undergo chemotherapy treatments. We had been at the hospital for about ten days when his kidneys shut down due to the chemotherapy treatments. Two days later his liver quit working as well. I remember when the Dr.came in and gave us the sad news that if Daddy's liver did not begin to work again that he was not gonna make it but a few more days. After the doctor left the room daddy made the comment: ***"Well son I might not make it"*** And that was it? That's all daddy had to say when faced with death. He never complained, Nor did he mention any regrets. Now that I am back in fellowship with my ***Lord and***

Savior Jesus Christ!! I understand how daddy was able to display such ***calmness,*** and ***peace*** when he ***faced death.***

I remember when daddy walked the aisle at Sanford first Baptist Church. And bro.Bill Nobles led daddy to ***Jesus!*** Daddy use to talk about ***Revelation.21:4- And God shall wipe away all tears from their eyes; and there shall be no more death, neither sorrow, nor crying, neither shall there be anymore pain: for the former things are passed away.***

Despite all the lessons I was taught as a kid, and going to church, and seeing my daddy ***Get Saved*** I still chose to follow Satan and the things of this world. I started ***Drinking*** at the age of ***Thirteen***. I was ***Arrested*** my first time on my ***Sixteenth birthday*** for public drunkenness. The downward spiral continued into ***Hard Drugs*** and all the pleasures of this world Satan has to offer. I could sit here and write page after page about all the things I have done before I was saved, but ***"God"*** has led me in no way to share my deeds of evil. Only to say that my adult life was spent in alcohol and drug addiction.

March 20th 2014: I was arrested in Perry county, ms. For possession with intent to distribute ***Crystal Meth,*** and possession of a controlled substance. Suddenly I was ***Facing*** the possibility of ***38 Years in state prison.*** The first month I was in jail, I was still blaming my problems on everyone except the man in the mirror. One night; I was laying on a thin mat, on the cold concrete floor of the jail cell. I was reminded of those ***Life lessons*** my daddy had taught me as a kid. How we should help our fellow man when we can,and how we shouldn't lie or steal, and It's always "***Better To make An Honest Living And Be poor;Than To Be Dishonest And Rich"*** And believe me; at the time I sure was regretting not taking my Daddy's advice about making an honest living! Then I began to think about daddy up there in heaven. Singing, laughing, and having a grand ole time. I thought about him looking down at me, and how disappointed he must have been to see me sitting in jail on drug charges. The idea of that softened my hard heart. I began to think about ***Heaven*** and ***Jesus!!*** and the profession of faith I had made 7 years prior to this moment. I realized it was time to quit blaming my problems on everyone else and accept responsibility for my actions. The most important thing I realized was my need to confess my sins to *"GOD"* and beg him to forgive me for my sins. I know I was forgiven for my sins because God's holy word tells me in. ***1 john-1:9- That if we confess our sins, he is faithful and just to forgive us our sins, and to cleanse us from all unrighteousness.***

I am so thankful I serve a merciful God. ***Eph. 2:4-But God, who is rich in mercy, for his great love wherewith he loved us,***

And a God who loves me enough to send his son to be beaten, mocked, and crucified!*"GOD"* not only sent ***Jesus!!*** to die for me but for all sinners; as we are told in ***Romans-5:8- But God commandeth his love toward us, in that,while we were yet sinners, Christ died for us.***

My time in the **Perry county jail** turned out to be a great blessing for me. There was plenty of time for me to read and **Study My Bible** and I kind of became the spiritual advisor in my cell block. I started a bible study and there was always four to five other men who would participate in the bible study. We started having a **Prayer circle**

Every night at lights out, and God was really doing a great work in my life and in the lives of some of the other men as well, once again; after the example set by my daddy. I started singing every night after we had our prayer circle. Daddy loved to sing; he use to sing at church, and he was ask to sing at several funerals, and family reunions. He was even singing from his hospital bed about two weeks before he died. I remember he use to tell people that he could stand up and sing in front of a thousand people and not be nervous one little bit!! but of course he was blind so he couldn't see the audience anyway. ***Lol!!*** This is just one example of how daddy never allowed his blindness to rob him of his joy in life. He could find the silver lining in every situation and bring happiness to the gloomiest of days. The good Lord knows I have my regrets about the way I lived my life. I would give anything to hold Daddy's hand and pray with him or sing a song with him at church but I wouldn't ask him to come back to this ole world for nothing. I know he's looking around heaven at the beauty that we can't even imagine. He's **Kicking Up Gold Dust On Those Streets Of Gold.** And singing bass in heavens choir. I can't wait to see him in heaven and worship our **Lord Jesus!!** together.

Now back to my stay at the Perry County jail. Every Tuesday a preacher named Herbert Wiggers would come and preach to us, and pray with us.

I really enjoyed hearing him preach and share the word with us. Brother Herbert would some times allow me to open up the service with a song. One day I was standing at the tray hole singing.(the tray hole is a 4x16 inch hole in the wall which allowed the guards to pass our food trays to us at mealtime) the guards would unlock the tray hole so we could hear bro.Herbert better out in the hallway. at this particular service Bro.Herbert ask me to sing at the end of the service and as I was singing; a new trustee walked up and placed a book in the tray hole and upon finishing my song I took the book and returned to my bunk. The following Tuesday when bro.Herbert returned, he ask me about the book? I assumed he had loaned it to me through the trustee. Bro. Herbert explained to me that while I was singing the trustee approached him and said*"Something"* told him to give the man singing the book and bro.Herbert also told me; as the trustee was returning from giving me the book. The trustee had tears streaming down his face from the ***Lord's*** conviction upon his heart. I make mention of this because at the time I was reading my bible; but I was a very young Christian. Although I had been saved 7 years prior. I did not do the things a young Christian should do to ***Survive The Wiles Of The Devil*** such as ***The Study Of The Bible*** so I had very little knowledge of the ***Bible*** this book was the "Illustrated bible hand book" by Lawrence O. Richards. The book contains commentary on a large number of the chapters in the ***Bible***

It is done in such a way that I can understand it. To receive this book was like having someone sit down with me, and answer my questions.

This is just one example of how ***"GOD PROVIDES FOR US"*** The exact things we need; at the exact time we need them. Through this book I was able to have a more in-depth ***Bible Study*** in my cell block.

I sometimes use the book when I give my testimony. And tell how the book was a gift from ***"GOD"*** we are given another example of how ***"GOD"*** provides for his people when Moses led Israel out of Egypt. ***Neh. 9:15- "And gavest them bread from***

heaven for their hunger, and broughtest forth water for them out of the rock for their thirst, and promisedst them that they should go in to possess the land which thou hast sworn to givedst them."

So I want to encourage you to keep plowing forward. **God Is A Faithful Provider For His Children** There's no doubt in my mind **God Will Provide** the things you need at the exact time you need them.

THE MAN IN THE CAGE:

This is the first poem I had written. as the title describes; I was the man in the cage. I was still in jail awaiting trial on drug charges. I was trying to describe the feeling of not only being in jail, but to be **Burdened with sin** and to have the sin choke out my joy and happiness. I also wanted to capture the peace and contentment that comes with **Knowing Jesus!! As Your Lord And Savior** and to have the protection of **Jesus!! And His Angels** around you all the time. After I confessed my sins and ask **"GOD"** to forgive me of my sins. I had an incredible feeling of peace; and I accepted the fact that I had broken the law and deserved to be punished. What I have trouble accepting is how many lives I have destroyed and families I have seen torn apart due to the drugs I was selling. I have watched people go from having a job, family and money in the bank to being completely strung out and broke; just trying to find their next high. I'm so thankful "***GOD" Delivered Me*** from alcohol and drugs. Many of my friends are still ***Junky's*** when I witness to them there's usually weed burning and whiskey bottles sitting on the table. I tell them about Jesus and how he's changed my life, and I ***Pray*** they can see the change in me and want to change as well. ***Pray For Me*** and the people I witness to that ***"GOD"*** will strengthen me and touch the lives of the people I witness to.

"The Man In The Cage"

I dreamt; of what I thought was an empty place.
Through a broken window I could see a lonely face?
As I walked closer no fear did I feel.
I gazed in and realized the lonely face was real!!
As our eye's met; I was in a state of disbelief?
His face was covered with torment and grief...
His heart was bound by sin and rage. And his body placed in a black iron cage...
At his back I could see the hounds of hell!
But he could not break free from his prison cell.
He began to cry, beg, and plead.
Then screamed;"Dear God; please set me free!!"
Behold there appeared a glorious sight.
It was **Jesus Christ!!** With ten thousand angels to his right!!
As **Jesus!!** Scattered the sin and rage.
I realized; I was the man in the cage.
Tim byrd 7.22.14

Psalm.103:12- As far as the east is from the west, so far hath he removed our transgressions from us.

OVER AN OVER AGAIN:

This poem describes the **constant cycle of Addiction,** And how addiction blinds a person. My **Downward spiral into addiction** happened so slow and gradual that I didn't realize I was addicted? To get drunk, or to get high became such a normal part of my life, that I didn't recognize it. Waking up in jail became a normal part of my life as well. I don't know how many times; I told myself and ask ***"GOD"*** "If you will get me out of this situation I'm in; I will never drink another drop or get high again". But it never failed as soon as I would get out of jail or get over the hang over of a week end drunk; I would go right back and do it again.

I am proud to say, March 21st 2014 was the last time I woke up in jail with a hang over; feeling

Helpless and Hopeless. I look back now, after 17 months of sobriety(which is the longest I have been sober my entire adult life) I realize how much of a ***Fool*** I was. I also know that ***Jesus!!*** Uses our past life to prepare us for the work he has for us to do in our future. No matter what kind of person you are or were ***Jesus!! Can use you*** in a mighty way! I once heard a man say, "We can only go as far as our ***Testimony*** takes us". Tell someone what ***Jesus!!*** Has done for you, and you just may be surprised by the way ***"GOD"*** uses your ***Testimony*** to encourage and change the lives of others.

"*Over An Over Again*"

It was late in the morning before I awoke.
From inside my cell; I could feel no hope.
Hope is the dream of a soul awake.
My dreams; last night's drinks did take.
Here I sit; broken, and sad, with all hope gone.
My head still pounds with last night's songs.
My mouth is dry; my hands are sweaty.
My stomach turns; from my nerves not being steady.
I kick myself over an over; and scream why again?
I know my addiction has me trapped in sin.
I search my soul hoping to find sobriety.
Then I realize my need for God Almighty.
Tim Byrd. 7.23.14

Pro.26:11- *As a dog returneth to his vomit, so a fool returns to his folly.*

THE LOVE OF A STRANGER:

This poem describes how **No Matter Who You Are** or what you have done. *"Jesus"* still loves you and wants you to **Know him as your Savior.** I must ask; ***Do you know Jesus?*** Not just the man **Jesus!!**

Who once walked the shores of Galilee, but do you know ***Jesus?? As The Son Of "GOD" And The Savior Of The World!!*** There's more to **Jesus!!** than just the Christmas story. I invite you to ***Come To Know Jesus!! As Your Savior!*** Even though you may not know him **He Knows You!** As a matter of fact he knows the very hairs on your head.

Matt.10:30- But the very hairs of your head are all numbered. And he loves you enough that he suffered the pain, and shame of **The Cross** for everyone to see. If **Jesus!!** is a stranger to you ***Your No Stranger To Him!***

"The Love Of A Stranger"

You loved me, before I was conceived. in your love I did not believe.
I lived my life with shame to hide.
Yet; you walked right by my side.
While my soul was evil and wrong.
My heart still heard your beautiful song.
As I came to know your love so divine.
You forever changed this heart of mine.
I was lost in sin; my heart was afraid.
Through your love; my soul was saved.
Now I'm complete; my soul is alive!
In your hands I will forever abide.
You cleansed my heart pure as snow.
Upon my face; a heavenly glow.
A lake of fire was my souls danger.
But I was saved by the love of a stranger.
Tim Byrd 7.23.14

> ***Jer. 1:5- Before I formed thee in the belly I knew thee; and before thou camest forth out of the womb I sanctified thee, and I ordained thee a prophet unto the nations.***

MY DADDY'S BROTHER:

This poem is about my *"Uncle Shimp"* there was six boys, two girls and a set of twins born to my grand parents Sam and Elmer Byrd. The twins were still born so of course I have no memory of them. The Byrd family worked as sharecroppers in the farm fields of Covington county around the small town of Seminary, Mr. Sam Byrd (my grandfather) died in 1958, at the age of 39 from lung cancer. My daddy was eight years old, and my uncle Shimp was nine years old when their daddy passed away. My grand mother: Elmer Byrd had the enormous task of raising 8 kids ranging from three years of age to fifteen years of age. The term "single parent" takes on a whole new meaning when your raising eight kids and your primary source of income is picking cotton during the summer and whatever you could find to do in the winter. My uncle Shimp told me he quit school in the third grade and went door to door looking for any kind of work someone would pay him to do so he could help his family survive. This was true with all the kids. My daddy quit school and went to work in the fourth grade. Anyone around my hometown who knew the Byrd family has the same common remark about Daddy and the way they grew up.*"-Those kids had it rough"* there was one year that separated daddy and my uncle Shimp. They were very close growing up and remained close as adults. I was always around my uncle Shimp and he was always very good to me. Him and his daughter Julie was the only visitors I had when I was locked up in Perry County as a matter of fact I wrote this poem after the first time they came to visit me. So I want to encourage you to spend a few more meals around the table with your family.*"GOD"* designed us to be family, and at the end of the day our family is what really matters.

  * I just want to point out; the line in this poem that reads*" more than once we have shared a drink"* refers to the time before I rededicated my life to *Jesus!!*

"My Daddy's Brother"

I know you were there the day I was born.
When you leave this world I will surely morn.
You and my daddy are from the same mother.
You are the favorite of my Daddy's brothers.
You have taught me many of life's lessons.
To have you as my uncle is truly a blessing.
More than once we have shared a drink.
As you gave me good advice or told me what you may think.
You never turned your back on me; despite what I had done.
You always treated me as if I was your own son.
We were together when daddy died.
On each others shoulder we both cried.
You have always been there; there will never be another.
I love and respect as much as my Daddy's Brother.
Tim Byrd 7.23.14

Pro.17:17- A friend loveth at all times, and a brother is born for adversity.

ALL THINGS NEW:

This is the last poem I had written before my release from the Perry County jail. I remember how excited I was about my upcoming court date, and finally being free again.

When your locked up all you can think about is what your gonna do when you get out. The things I was planning on doing was different this time. I was planning on getting back in church and **Living My Life For Jesus!!** the way I should have when I got saved in 2007. Now that I had received forgiveness for my sins and my turning away from the lord. I was bound and determined not to go back to my **Old Ways** and with the help of **Jesus!!** I am still **Dedicated to my lord and Savior** and living a dedicated Christian life. I still have struggles and there's still things and people I see that triggers my desire to get drunk or get high. I sometimes still get mad but I am learning more everyday how to control my emotions and deal with the desires of my addictions. As Christians **Our Prayer Life** is a crucial part of our battle with Satan and his demons. Our prayers are the one thing that Satan can not touch!! Through **Jesus Christ!!** And his **Death On The Cross** we have open access to the creator of the universe. Our prayers are very powerful and necessary to win our daily battles! Please keep me in your prayers and pray that **"GOD"** will continue to strengthen me and use me in some way to further "**The Kingdom Of Heaven**"

"ALL THINGS NEW"

Here I sit; with my time almost gone.
In less than a week I should be home.
I have welcomed this week for such a long time.
As my journey continues; freedom will soon be mine.
I sit and dream of the things I want to do.
And my mind orbits around all things new.
To the man I was I shall never return.
My fire for Jesus shall always burn.
He has provided me joy; and peace for tomorrow.
I'm no longer held captive by sorrow.
From behind these bars I shall soon be free.
My love for Jesus shall go with me.
The old me; I will leave in this lonely cell.
Because the new me is alive and doing well.
Tim Byrd 8.23.14

2 Cor .5:17- therefore if any man be in Christ, he is a new creature: old things are passed away; behold, all things are become new.

HEAR MY PRAYER:

The first line of this poem is also the first line of ***Psalm.39:12.*** And like the ***Psalm.39:12***
This is my prayer to *"GOD"* to save the lost souls.

My greatest desire is to see as many as possible come to **Know Jesus!! As Lord And Savior.** And to tell people about **Jesus!!** And what he has done in my life. I love to share my testimony. when I witness to people or pray with them. and I can see the **Holy Spirit** working in their heart it gives me an incredible feeling of joy, and satisfaction. I work in the bus ministry at Sanford first Baptist Church. Part of the ministry is going out witnessing, and inviting people to church. It is sometimes discouraging when I go canvas an area, and people shut the door in your face, or say they have no need for church; but when i witness to someone and they receive **"God's"** word and I can see the power of **"God's" Holy Spirit** working in their heart, it just feeds my spirit,and sparks the fire ***Jesus!!*** Has put in my heart to lead people to ***Jesus!!.*** I was once told that I couldn't charge hell with a water pistol, and I replied, ***"I Can Charge Hell With a Water Pistol Because I Have The Living Water In My Pistol!!"***

When "***GOD***" tells me in ***Phill. 4:13- I can do all things through Christ which strenghteneth me.***

I believe every word of it. We were not called to sit on the church pew and eat big meals in the fellowship hall! We were called to be witnesses for our **Lord Jesus!!.** If your not sure about "***GODS" Will For Your Life.***Just look on the next page and read ***Mark.16:15.***

"HEAR MY PRAYER"

Hear my prayer oh lord, and give ear unto my cry.
Receive my words; save the lost before they die.
Cleanse their soul from your thrown so divine.
Save them from he who awaits as a hungry lion.
I come before you with a humble heart.
Convict their souls; bring forth a brand new start.
Only you lord can hear my tearful prayer.
Please save the lost; give them your love and care.
Take from them all their earthly desire.
And save them from Lucifer's lake of fire.
Tim Byrd 10.17.14

> ***Mark 16:15- And he said unto them, Go ye into all the world and preach the gospel to every creature***
>
> ***16:20- and they went forth, and preached everywhere, The lord working with them, and confirming the word with signs following. Amen.***

BELIEVE:

This poem describes the simplicity of coming to know **Jesus!!** As your **Personal Savior.** It's as simple as **Believing** and **Asking.**

Romans 10:9-That if thou shalt confess with thy mouth the Lord Jesus,

And shalt believe in thine heart that God hath raised him from the dead, thou shalt be saved.

10:10- For with the heart man believeth unto righteousness; and with the mouth confession is made unto salvation. This poem also describes the personal relationship **Jesus!!** Wants to have with each and every one of us. **Jesus!!** Is capable of loving us all as if we're his only child. His love is always searching for his lost sheep.

Matt 18:11- For the son of man is come to save that which was lost.

18:12- How think ye? If a man have a hundred sheep, and one of them be gone astray, doth he not leave the ninety and nine and goeth into the mountains, and seeketh that which is gone astray? If you don't know *Jesus!!* As your *Lord And Savior;* I invite you to *Believe on the Lord Jesus!!* And become the person *Jesus!!* wants you to be.

Acts 16:31: And they said believe on the lord Jesus Christ, and thou shalt be saved, and thy house.

"BELIEVE"

I envisioned a place no one could see.
Where it was only Jesus and me.
He spoke as if I was his only child.
Said he had waited for such a long while.
He explained how he was never really hid.
And there was no need to suffer as I did.
He showed me holes in his hands; said in him I could trust.
And how he had suffered enough for all of us.
He took me high upon a hill called Calvary.
Said he was nailed to a cross for you and me.
These things he told me; I could not yet conceive?
Then he said my child; "all you have to do is believe"
Tim Byrd 10-20-14

Hebrews 11:6- But without faith it is impossible to please him: for he that cometh to God must believe that he is, and that he is a rewarder of them that diligently seek him.

FIERY TRIALS:

As Christians we all experience trials, tribulation and temptations. ***Jesus!!*** Was tempted by the devil for 40 days. For us to expect not to be tempted is foolish?

Luke 4:2- Being forty days tempted of the devil. And in those days he did eat nothing: and when they were ended, he afterward hungered. Not only should we expect to be tempted but we are to rejoice in our temptations. ***1 Peter 1:6- wherein we greatly rejoice, though now for a season, if need be, ye are in heaviness through manifold temptations:***

1:7- That the trial of your faith being much more precious than of gold that perisheth, though it be tried with fire, might be found unto praise and honor and glory at the appearing

of Jesus Christ: before we were saved and living in sin

We couldn't even recognize the sin in our life because we didn't have the ***"Holy Spirit"*** living in our heart to convict us of sin. Our Christian walk is not always gonna be a mountain top experience but down in the valley is where the green grass grows and the calm waters flow. Our temptations are designed to make us ***"Stronger Soldiers For Jesus!!"***

If we cast our troubles on ***Jesus!!*** We will win our battles. ***John 16:33- These things I have spoken unto you, that in me ye might have peace. In the world ye shall have tribulation: but be of good cheer; I have over come the world.*** Upon my release from jail in Perry County on Aug.28th 2014. I had no choice but to move back to the same place I was living when I was arrested. All of a sudden I was surrounded by alcohol,drugs, and all the things I was doing prior to my arrest. It wasn't long before all my old dope buddies,and girlfriends was knocking on my door again. This was a very difficult time for me. Satan was coming against me in a very powerful way but I was able to resist my temptations through

Fasting And Prayer and allowing *"GOD"* to speak to me through ***the Bible.*** I became completely dependent on *"GOD"* to deliver me from these temptations. It's hard for me to describe what was taking place inside of me; my soul felt like a war zone. I kept thinking about ***James 4:7- Submit yourselves therefore to God. Resist the devil and he will flee from you. 4:8- Draw nigh to God and he will draw nigh to you. Cleanse your hands, ye sinners; and purify your hearts, ye double minded.***

As I continued in prayer I experienced the presence of *"GOD"* to the point that my feet were burning, not burning like I was standing on hot coals, but a warming sensation on the inside of my body; especially in the pads of my feet. A pastor I told of my experience told me that I was standing on holy ground and *"GODS"* presence had created a holy environment around me.

I'm not prepared to explain what happened to me that day, but I will say that things happen when we experience *"GODS" Presence. **Souls are saved, bodies are healed, and joy and happiness abounds!! From the presence of "GOD"***

"FIERY TRIALS"

As we experience fiery trials, struggles and pain.
We turn from God and begin to complain.
From fiery trials we can always learn a lesson.
Then fiery trials becomes another of God's blessings.
We must be eager to learn and in God we must grow.
As we take victory over Satan God's love will show.
Without trials we would never achieve confidence.
Nor learn to trust in God and what he represents.
So never give up, and never give in.
The fight is fixed, and your gonna win!
God provides love,and peace; which makes us content.
Grace, and mercy are also heaven sent.
When times are tough, and you see no end.
Just call on Jesus, and take victory once again.
Tim Byrd 10.25.14

Matt.11:28- come unto me, all ye that labor and are heavy laden, and I will give you rest.

11:29- take my yolk upon you, and learn of me; for I am meek and lowly in heart: and ye shall find rest unto your souls.

NEVER LOSE SIGHT:

This poem describes the price ***Jesus!!*** Paid so that we as sinners can be forgiven for our sins. ***John 1:29- the next day John seeth Jesus coming unto him, and saith Behold the Lamb of God, which taketh away the sin of the world.***

And how ***Jesus!!*** Stepped down from the splendor of his thrown in heaven to be born in a manger here on earth. ***Phil.2:6- who being in the form of God, thought it not robbery to be equal with God 2:7- But made himself of no reputation, and took upon him the form of a servant, and was made in the likeness of men: 2:8- and being found in fashion as a man, he humbled himself and became obedient unto death, even the death of the cross.***

It's hard for me to imagine **How Violent This Day Was For Jesus...**

Not only was he nailed to the cross, and put up to bleed out, and suffer the elements of mother nature, but every person who was sentenced to the Roman crucifixion received a **Scourging.** Which is the same as a flogging. This was done with the **Cat Of Nine Tails.** Which would be laced with **Bits Of Metal And Shards Of Bone**

The weight of the bits of metal would create deep bruising and the Shards of bone would help cut the flesh to ribbons. ***Matt.27:26- Then released he Barrabbas unto them: and when he had scourged Jesus , he delivered him to be crucified.***

27:30- And they spit upon him, and took the Reed, and smote him on the head. Not only was our Lord ***Jesus!!*** Beat in the head with a stick. He was also mocked, and humiliated.

John 19:2- And the Soldiers plaited a crown of thorns, and put it on his head, and they put on him a purple robe, 19:3- And said, Hail, King of the Jews! and they smote him with their hands.

This term "they smote him with their hands" does not fully describe what really took place. The Roman soldiers played a game with **_Jesus!!_** Called **_Hot hands._** With **_Jesus!!_** Being blind folded. The Roman soldiers would take turns hitting **_Jesus!!_** In the face with the palms of their hands. Upon removal of the blind fold the Soldiers would mockingly ask **_Jesus!!_** To choose which soldier did not participate in hitting him in the face. We are given a description of the abuse in **_Isaiah 53:14- As many were astonished at thee; his visage was so marred more than any man, and his form more than the sons of men:_** It has been estimated the romans crucified up to 30,000 people a year. To say that **_Jesus!!_** Was marred more than any other man is a profound statement of the abuse **_Jesus!! Suffered for me and you._** The love Jesus displayed for us by **_taking our place on the cross_** should be enough to melt the hardest of hearts, and encourage every human to want to **_Know Jesus!! As Lord And Savior._**

Our Lord **_Jesus!!_** Not only suffered unspeakable physical sufferings;but we can not imagine nor describe the mental anguish he must have suffered on the cross. We have **_"God's" Promise_** that he will never leave us or forsake us. ***Deaut. 31:6- Be strong and of a good courage, fear not, nor be afraid of them: for the lord thy God, he it is that doth go with thee;he will not fail thee, nor forsake thee.***

However **Jesus!!** Was orphaned by **"GOD"** on the cross, and suffered the wrath of his own father as our sins, and the sins of the world was poured out on **Jesus!!**

Psalm 22:1- My God, my God, why hast thou forsaken me? Why art thou so far from helping me, and from the words of my roaring?

The great apostle Paul tells us that **Jesus!!** Became sin for us in

2 Cor. 5:21- For he hath made him to be sin for us, who knew no sin; that we might be made the righteousness of God in him.

If your a **Lost person** and don't know **Jesus!! As your lord and savior.** I want you to pause for a minute, and just think about the **Price Jesus!! Paid**

So you can enjoy the freedom of salvation and the rewards of a **Christ Filled Life!** And remember your **Not Promised Tomorrow.** Today is a great day to secure your spot in heaven.

The bible tells us that now is the time of salvation. ***2 Cor. 6:2- For he saith, I have heard thee in a time accepted, and in the day of salvation have I succored thee: behold, now is the day of salvation.***

"NEVER LOSE SIGHT"

I dreamt of a tall foggy hill.
Where it was quiet, calm, and still.
As my eyes took a look around.
My ears heard an Erie sound.
The calm was shattered by a hammer and nail.
I heard agony in a man's yell.
My heart dropped and my senses soared.
As I heard the hammer strike once more.
My curiosity would not let me be.
I started up a hill called Calvary.
As I reached the top; I could not believe my eyes?
The calm was replaced with screams and cries.
I saw three men being crucified.
There was one the Soldiers seemed to despise.
Yet he said; "forgive them father, they know not what they do."
And I read these words; The King of The Jews.
As he raised his head and took his last breath.
The earth began to shake upon his death.
The skies turned black, and the wind was a stir!
Then all of a sudden my dream was a blur?
As my vision returned, a tomb I could see!
The man from the cross was in front of me?

He said ; "hello my child; Jesus is my name"
"You don't know me; but I love you just the same"
"For your sins; with my life I have paid."
"Risen from my grave to show you the way"
"My father in heaven loves you as well"
"Let me save you from the fires of hell"
As I stared in his eyes; the cross I could see.
Then salvation was given to me.
He died for me; while I was lost.
Now I pray to never lose sight of the cross.
Tim Byrd 11.16.14

THE MISSION:

This poem is about the *"Mission At The Cross"* in Laurel, MS..

The Mission is a faith based Drug rehabilitation facility for men.

The Mission and the *Hellfighters Motor Cycle Ministry* was founded by **Richard And Gina Headrick.**

I was released from Perry County jail on Aug.28th 2014. I was accepted at *The mission* two months later on Oct.29th. My acceptance at *The Mission* was a great blessing for me. I was able to get out of the drug filled environment I was living in.

I'm proud to say I completed the program at *The Mission* on April 29th 2015. I have also completed my 16 month probation period with the *Mississippi Department Of Corrections*. In December of 2015. I hope within a year I can have my fines paid and have my drivers license back. Please continue to pray for me.

"*THE MISSION*"

Dawn is cracking as I leave from the bridge.
All-night I seen the red Cross just over the ridge.
I have a long walk but hope is what I see.
I've gotten use to those who point and stare at me.
Hunger has fueled my latest decision.
I hope they will accept me down at the mission.
As I hit the street a car speeds past.
I hoped they would stop; but hope fades fast.
A life of addiction is what got me here.
My soul is bitter, has no cheer.
I think of my family; tears fill my eyes.
I already know there's no need to cry.
I step up my pace to fight off the cold.
The frost I feel is down in my soul.
I never thought this would happen to me.
Homeless is not what I drempt to be.
My body is sore from my nights on the ground.
I'm almost at the mission; I can't slow down.
The day has passed; I have finally arrived.
I must keep the courage to step inside.
I swallow my pride and continue to walk.
A man warmly greets me;we begin to talk.
I notice something about him I usually don't see.

It seems he actually cares about me?
He invites me in, and says "Please have a seat."
Before I know it; he brings me something to eat.
My first night there I slept very good.
I felt comfortable; not so misunderstood.
The next morning I met Jesus during devotion.
God's plan for me was set into motion.
A year has passed, and I'm still clean.
To walk with Jesus is my new dream.
God has blessed me with a new life.
Forgiveness I have received from my wife.
I sit and watch my children play.
These words are all I can say.
God bless the day I made the decision.
To walk through those doors down at the mission.
Tim Byrd 11.22.14

Today **10-4-15** was a **Land Mark Day** for me as I made my public surrender to ministry. I've known *"GOD" Called Me To Be An Evangelist.* For about a year now. I waited so long to accept it because I just didn't believe *"GOD"* would use someone like me to preach his word.

I never thought I was a good enough person to be a preacher? The truth is I'm not a good enough person to preach the gospel; but neither was Paul or Peter; *"Jesus Christ"* was the only man ever good enough to preach the **Word Of "GOD"**. when we are baptized into the body of Christ we are given the ability and power to do what "**GOD**" has called us to do.

I have no doubt, *I'm the most unlikely preacher ever!* But I'm being obedient to the calling of my **Lord And Savior.** And taking the alter by the horns, and from this day forward, *I'm A Preacher!* A dear friend of mine told me something that makes perfect sense, and it's completely true. ***"GOD" Doesn't Call Those Who Are Equipped... He Equips Those Who Are Called!!*** As always I want to encourage you to step up to the calling ***"GOD"*** has placed on you!

A SINNER LIKE ME:

In this poem i was thinking about the life ***Jesus!!*** Deserved to live compared to the life he chose to live. The thought that really stuck in my mind was the fact that ***Jesus!!*** Was a carpenter. ***Mark.6:3- Is not this the carpenter, the son of Mary, the brother of James, and Joses, and of Judah, and Simon? And are not his sisters here with us? And they were offended at him.*** I am under the belief that every time ***Jesus!!*** drove a nail into a piece of wood he had to think about his day on Calvary, and the way he was gonna die. Yet as his ministry started all he wanted to do was perform the will of his father and preach,and teach others about the kingdom of heaven, and bring joy and happiness to those he came in contact with. In the gospel of John when ***Jesus!!*** Washed the disciples feet. ***Jesus!!*** Knew Judas Iscariot was gonna betray him, yet ***Jesus!!*** Washed the feet of Judas anyway. ***John.13:2- And supper being ended, the devil having now put into the heart of Judas Iscariot, Simon's son to betray him.***

13:4- He riseth from supper,and laid aside his garments; and took a towel and girded himself.

13:5-After that he poureth water into a basin,and began to wash the disciples' feet, and to wipe them with the towel wherewith he was girded.

13:11- For he knew who should betray him; therefore said he, ye are not all clean

I pray that as my walk with ***Jesus!!*** Continues that I can grow to truly

Love people the way ***Jesus!!*** did and live up to the commandment he gives us in ***John.13:34- A new commandment I give unto you, That ye love one another as I have loved you, that ye also love one another.***

13:35- By this shall all men know that ye are my disciples,if ye have love one to another.

"A SINNER LIKE ME"

I sit and wonder of the things Jesus knew.
The extremes he would go and the things he would do.
He began his life from a virgin birth.
Born in a manger he didn't deserve.
By way of David he could have been king.
The kingdom of heaven is all he foreseen.
He was sent by God among us to dwell.
Was found teaching at the age of twelve.
As he grew in wisdom, and stature.
He became the man that no one could measure.
He performed many miracles for people to see.
In and around the town of Galilee.
He taught us to love and have a cheerful heart.
Although he seen his death from the very start.
He always knew how his life would end.
His life he gave to free us from sin.
The sting of death he did not feel.
With a thousand tongue's I could never reveal.
How thankful I am that he rose from his grave.
So a sinner like me could come to be saved.
Tim Byrd 1.16.15

Continuing strength international ministries: As I mentioned in the dedication. I am writing this book to help fund ***"Continuing Strength International Ministries"*** myself and bro.Raju amruthapudi are partners in this small ministry of the lord. I am honored to be part of ***Continuing Strength International Ministries*** with bro. Raj. Bro.Raj is a man on fire for ***Jesus!!*** In his country of ***India***.

Bro. Raj and his associates have created and developed ***the Pastoral training institute*** in ***vinukonda, Andrapradesh India.***

Bro. Raj provides accommodations,supplies,and meals to the students of the school. ***The Pastoral Training Institute And planting christian church's*** is our main focus point. The school is only open, and training pastors in the beginning months of the year. Due to insufficient funds. We believe that the training of new pastors is the most important step in the process of spreading ***"God's Word In the country of India"*** the country of ***India*** has a population of ***1.27 billion people.*** Of this large population only ***2 percent are Christian,*** with ***80 percent being Hindu*** and ***15 percent being Muslim.*** So there's a great need for properly trained pastors to **plant Christian Church's in the country of India.**

Bro.raj is also active in spreading the gospel in the public school system. Many of the schools will not allow him to speak to the students however in 2015 bro raj. Was able to speak to about 1,500 Students and provide Students with toys,candy or some other type of loving gift. Our vision for the future is to create and develop an orphanage for 10 children. ***PLEASE PRAY FOR THIS MINISTRY!!***

Bro.Raj and I have been friends for more than a year now. We are in constant contact with one another. He has been a great blessing to me, and a wonderful mentor. I am truly thankful to have bro. Raj as my **Brother in Christ,** And my ministry partner.

More than once I have been chatting with bro. Raj. while he was traveling all night by bus to some remote village to spread the gospel.One time bro. Raj. had traveled all-night to a remote location he described as **The Wilderness.** That night he slept out on the ground exposed to the elements,- mosquito's, and whatever kind of other bugs, and critters that may be in a Wilderness of india? My point is however that bro. Raj. Goes anywhere he is invited or led by the spirit to go. I'm convinced

"God" did not give me the gift of poetry, just to have the poems in a notebook sitting on the shelf collecting dust. I feel with my whole heart this is what ***"God"*** wants me to do. Bro.Raj has invited me to come to India and preach the word with him. it is my prayer God will allow me the honor of actually going to the country of india. I'm sure the good people of bro.Raj's church has never met an actual ***Redneck!!*** Lol!! Bro.raj tells me his wife ***Leelavathi*** is a great cook and they love spicy food! I tell him that here in the south we love good cooking and that where two or more Baptist are gathered together a chicken has to die!! Because we love to get together and eat.

On a serious note, I ***THANK YOU!!*** For your prayers and support of this small ministry, and always remember ***Jesus!! Started with twelve!!***

Testimony of Raju Amruthapudi:

Praise the lord!

I am praising God who has given me this opportunity to share my testimony; once again with you, and secondly I would like to thank you all who are encouraging me in Christ.

Birth And Childhood:

This is pastor Raju Amruthapudi. Who was born to my parents as a first fruit.

I was grown up with good discipline as others. I was an obedient of my parents till my tenth standard.

After getting out for the college I got into bad companies. I did not care the words of my parents though they warned me often.

Youth and salvation: in my college days I use to roam around with my friends. Slowly the bad habits such as drinking, and smoking developed in me. In other hand my parents always warns me about my changing behavior. One day my mom ask me to come to a gospel meeting nearby home. I agreed to follow her just for that day only cause I was in a bit distress. That day I heard the gospel of lord Jesus Christ and there was no peace in my heart. So went around my friends to get the peace of mind but no peace I got from them. And then I approached a pastor,and he said the lord is started his work in me and he ask to pray. I knelt down though I don't know how to pray. The tears are rolling down and my personal sins started to scroll before me while I was praying. That night a voice said to me; confess everything I will wipe them. I then realized that was the voice of the lord, and I started to attend the church.

Call for the ministry: God called me in a special way. After my conversion I was like a church going believer and I was on trails to get a good job. I told to my friends to enquire about a job. One day I had slept after praying. I had a dream. In that dream I was sitting and chatting with my friends, suddenly an old man approached me and asked me what I was doing there. I said; I simply sat? then this old man told me that all of your friends has their jobs but you have a different job by saying this he ask me to follow him to find the job which he was going to show me. I just followed him. He then took me into a field and given me an iron rod, and ask me to take out the weeds. Then he told me that he will come back to see my work. I did not understand the meaning of it so I went to my pastor to explain the dream.after hearing all that my pastor told me. that God is calling you for the ministry to work for him.(and he explained the meaning. Field is signifying the church and iron rod is signifying God's word) so I obeyed the call and decided to go to bible collage to equip myself with God's word. And I had my graduation in biblical studies.

Ministry: after I back from bible collage. I worked for two years and started to work in a town called Vinukonda. I started with three of my family members. But God blessed this church with thirty people of God. After three years God lead me to village where there is no church. All the village who are living as agricultural laborer's. There also started with few children. Now God lead more than twenty people. I am not satisfied with what I am doing so I prayed and started weekend evangelism once in a day . this is on Saturday. And visiting the bus stands,market places,and hospitals once in a week. After some time God inspired me to start a school of evangelism where few youngsters and evangelist are studying and meditating together. Please pray for this small ministry of the lord.

Yours faithfully
Raju Amruthapudi.
Raju & Leelavathi Amruthapudi
rajleelaevangelicalmission@gmail.com

Pastor at way to life full gospel church
Vinukonda, Andrapradesh India
Studied at Rhema Bible Training College
Lives in Goa,India
From: Darsi, Andrapradesh. India
Born- January 14th 1984
Cell- +919704370866
Founding member of The Pastoral Training Institute located in Vinukonda, Andrapredesh. India.

A CHILD OF MINE:

I wrote this poem while I was at The Mission At the Cross. Part of being an alcoholic and a junky is the fact I had never learned how to deal with my emotions, and the problems of life. I dealt with my problems by getting drunk or high so I never developed any real communication skills. **My answer to problems was usually violence.** I thought a man was measured by how tough he was or who he could beat up.

Violence was always a part of selling drugs. I still see people who I have hurt in the past. some of them accept my apology, and some of them don't. I received a great compliment recently. A child hood friend told me that when he heard I had gotten saved and changed my life that he thought it was only a cover up and didn't really believe it;

but after being around me for a week on the job he could tell that I had truly changed. My temper and my violent nature is probably the biggest change that has taken place in my life. The love **_Jesus!!_** Has shown me is the same love I try to show to others. The **_Love Of Christ!_** Is definitely something we all need.

"A CHILD OF MINE"

All at once I'm no longer humble, and meek.
As Lucifer sets upon me and sifts me as wheat.
I put on my armor and begin my prayer.
I connect with Jesus, and upon his face I stare.
I hear Jesus say: "my child; there's no need to doubt"
With a voice of thunder I hear Jesus shout.
" Bow before me Satan. This is a child of mine!"
"Release the chains you have placed on his mind!"
"I command you Satan with the power of my thrown"
"To depart from my child, and leave him alone."
As I feel my mind being set free.
I remember the price Jesus paid for me.
As he calmly wipes the tears from my face.
I feel the love and warmth of his embrace.
Then he says; "my child; for you I am always here"
"Put away your doubt and all of your fear."
"I have been here for you since the beginning of time."
"Always remember; you are a child of mine"
Tim Byrd 1.20.15

Eph. 4:31- Let all bitterness, and wrath, and anger, and clamor be put away from you, with all malice:

4:32- And be ye kind one to another,- tender hearted, forgiving one another even as God for Christ sake has forgiven you.

SOLDIER OF THE CROSS:

I wrote this poem about **Bro.Gene Douglas.** Bro. Gene is the pastor at **Highland Baptist Church** in Laurel MS. Highland Baptist is the home church of **The Mission At The Cross.** Bro.Gene and the other members of highland Baptist are a true blessing to me and the other men that go through the program at "The mission" I truly enjoyed hearing Bro. Gene preach the word of **"GOD"**

The hospitality and fellowship given to me and the men from the mission by the members of highland baptist was second to none. I was even allowed to sing in the choir under the direction of

Bro. Tony Harmon. I want to take this opportunity to thank Bro.Gene and Bro.Tony and all the members of Highland Baptist Church for accepting me and making me feel at home.

"SOLDIER OF THE CROSS"

He stood in the pulpit with a mighty glare.
Eyes fixed on Jesus with a steady stare.
He preached with passion to every man.
A soldier of the cross, Bible in hand.
Never once did he have reason for fears.
But more than once he shed many tears.
He preached the word with inspiring love.
He was a servant to our Lord jesus above.
He proclaimed Jesus with a mighty tongue of fire.
Saving souls from hell was his greatest desire.
He led his flock with the sound of his voice.
Preached the cross as the only choice.
He often said; "Laviticans put away your knives!"
The Lamb of God has paid the price for our lives.
It seemed his wife Brenda was his biggest fan.
The two of them were often seen hand in hand.
He poured out his heart every sermon I seen.
He was a soldier of the cross named bro.Gene.
Tim Byrd 2.1.15

Romans 10:13- For whosoever shall call on the name of the lord shall be saved.

10:14- How then shall they call on him in whom they have not believed? and how shall they believe in him of whom they have not heard? and how shall they hear without a preacher?

HEART OF STONE:

This poem is about the way I felt when I got saved. I accepted **_Jesus!!_** As my lord and savior in April of 2007. As I had previously mentioned. My daddy took me to church as a kid, and I knew about **_Jesus!!_** But I still chose to chase the way of the world and not listen to my daddy. I really got to thinking about **_Jesus!!_** After the death of my best friend **Chris Mixon** due to a drug over dose. Chris's death really got me to thinking about how precious life really was. However the death of Chris was not enough to bring me to **_Jesus!._**

A couple of week's after Chris's death I went out to the local bar.got drunk, and wrecked my girlfriends car on the way home. I was knocked out for a couple of hours from the wreck. When I woke up it was pouring down rain, and i proceeded to walk home in the rain. Of course my girlfriend was furious. Although we had been together for ten years this was the last straw for her, and I don't blame her. I woke up the next day with a severe hang over, broken ribs, a broken collar bone, A cracked sternum, a busted head, no vehicle,and no girlfriend. Believe me when I tell you ***It Was A Bad Morning!!***

But the thing I couldn't quit thinking about was the fact that if I would have died in the wreck I would have woke up in hell! So I got down on my knee's

Right there in my living room floor, and poured my heart out to ***Jesus!!*** I asked ***Jesus!!*** To forgive me of my sins and to come into my heart. I guess for ten or fifteen minutes I wept before the lord, and realized what kind of wretched person I had been. When I stood to my feet I was a new man. The thing I remember most is I felt as though an enormous weight had been lifted off of me. I was content with my situation, and I had peace in my heart.

Despite my situation I was actually happy! I started going to church and attending a bible study. I continued living a sober Christian life for about 8 months which was the longest I had been sober my entire adult life. I was able to get a job with a company named Oceaneering. I worked on the deck of a ship as a rigger; which means I would hook things up to the crane to be lowered to the sea floor or assist in completing crane operations. I went out on a brand new 450 foot ship, and decided to stay out as long as possible. I ended up being out to sea for three months. during this time I was not studying my bible or praying or any of the things a Christian should do to stay a strong devoted Christian. There was not many Christians on the ship, and all the other men talked about was the things of the world they were gonna do when they got home. After three months I decided to go home. on my way back to Mississippi I stopped in slidell, La. And got me a six pack of Budweiser. That's all it took to get me back in the grip of addiction. once again I was caught in the snare of Satan. It wasn't to many weeks I failed a drug test and lost my job. I returned back to the drug business and continued this life style for the next seven years until my arrest in Perry county. It's ironic the way things turned out. A great offshore job turned out to be my downfall, and my arrest on drug charges turned out to be a great blessing. I'm convinced Satan's greatest trick is to convince people their saved when their not or to make the true Christians ineffective as soul winner's for the kingdom of heaven.

"*HEART OF STONE*"

Satan had me convinced I would always be alone.
I would never be free from my heart of stone.
The weight of my addiction had me chained and bound.
Eternity in hell was my future crown.
I never thought Jesus would love someone like me.
The day we met my soul was set free.
My heart of stone was instantly shattered.
Life was forever changed as my sins were scattered.
The warmth of Jesus flowing through my soul.
Felt as though my skin was about to glow.
As the weight of sin was taken from me.
It felt as though I was given wings.
The flow of Jesus set my soul on fire.
To tell others of Jesus is my new desire.
Now I speak from a heart that's true.
What Jesus done for me; he wants to do for you.
You too can hear the angels sing their song.
Just ask Jesus to bust your heart of stone.
Tim Byrd 2.10.15

Ezek. 36:26- A new heart also will I give you, and a new spirit will I put within you: and I will take away the stony heart out of your flesh, and I will give you a heart of flesh.

THE YOUNG PREACHER:

This poem is about me? I wanted to describe the way I feel when I'm standing in the pulpit. However I don't think words can accurately describe the feeling I get when I am filled with the holy spirit, and my adrenaline is pumping, and I'm under the influence of the holy spirit.

I want you to understand; it's not fear that I feel. As Christians we do not possess the spirit of fear is what Paul tells a young preacher by the name of timothy in *2 Timothy 1:7- For God has not given us the spirit of fear; but of power, and of love, and of a sound mind.*

When I'm in the pulpit; I'm happy beyond measure, my energy level goes through the roof, my nerves will have my knee's knocking, yet my heart is broken because I'm presenting *Jesus!!*

To possible lost souls, and defeated christians with the hope that the lost will get saved, and the defeated take victory in *Jesus!!*

I need to add that I have not yet preached a sermon in which more than a hundred have come to be saved as the last line of this poem suggest. I have been blessed enough to see people get saved or rededicate their lives to *Jesus!!*

1 John 4:18- There is no fear in love; but perfect love casteth out fear: because fear hath torment. He that feareth is not made perfect in love.

"THE YOUNG PREACHER"

I stood in the pulpit with trembling knee's.
Calling on the lord; "help me please."
God heard my prayer and gave a reply.
"Don't worry my child; I'm right by your side."
"Remember my promise to always be true."
"You can depend on me, I'm gonna see you thru."
Then I remembered the day I was saved.
Thought of the price Jesus had paid.
I drew a deep breath; and began my sermon.
It was a message from God that left hearts burning.
I preached about Jesus, and his day on the cross.
My words brought conviction to all who were lost.
The kingdom of heaven was extended that day.
As more than a hundred came to be saved.
Tim Byrd 2.23.15

> *Col.4:3- Withal praying also for us, that God would open unto us a door of utterance, to speak the mystery of Christ, for which also I am in bonds:*
>
> *4:4- That I may make it manifest as I ought to speak.*

"HE SEES ME"

What kind of man would I be.
If I'm the man Jesus can't see?
I would be a man of sorrow and grief.
Destined to the fires of hell with no relief.
I would be a man desolate and alone.
Hope and peace would also be gone.
I would be a man of violence and war.
The joy of salvation would be no more.
I'm thankful today that Christ died for me.
I know my heart Jesus can see.
He sees me when I'm scared, and afraid.
He seen me even before I was saved.
He seen me as his precious child.
Even when my heart was evil,and wild.
I know my heart Jesus can see.
Because of the price he paid on Calvary.
Tim Byrd 3.11.15.

Romans.8:27- And he that searcheth the hearts knoweth what is the mind of the spirit, because he maketh intercession for the saints according to the will of God.

1cor.2:10- But God hath revealed them to us by his spirit: for the spirit searcheth all things, yea, the deep things of God.

2:12- Now we have received, not the spirit of the world, but the spirit which is of God; that we might know the things that are freely given to us of God.

2:14- but the natural man receiveth not the things of the spirit of God: for they are foolishness unto him: neither can he know them, because they are spiritually discerned.

2:15- but he that is spiritual judgeth all things, yet he himself is judged of no man.

"GRIEF TO GLORY"

My words can not express the way that I feel.
To be part of something God has made real.
My past life I was Satan's mighty tool.
He deceived me with pleasures and made me his fool.
He ruled my life with the wave of his hand.
Kept me blinded from God's mighty plan.
Prison was the life Satan made for me.
Until God came down to set me free.
Now I know that my life is complete.
I'm no longer violent but humble and meek.
God has saved me from the prince of the air.
He's made me whole with his love and care.
I use my words to tell the wonderful story.
Of how my life was changed from grief to glory.
Tim Byrd 4.11.15

Rom.8:18- for I reckon that the sufferings of this present time are not worthy to be compared with the glory which shall be revealed in us.

8:21- because the creature itself also shall be delivered from the bondage of corruption into the glorious liberty of the children of God.

John.17:24- Father I will that they also, whom thou hast given me, be with me where I am; that they may behold my glory, which thou hast given me: for thou lovedst me before the foundation of the world.

MY DAY ON CALVARY:

This poem I had written one day while I was reflecting back on the great achievements I was able to accomplish through the strength of my renewed relationship with **Jesus!!** My sobriety is one of those accomplishments. When I wrote this poem I had been sober for the first year of my adult life. Today is Jan.3rd 2016 and I look forward to another sober year,and a good year for the ministry "**GOD"** has blessed me with.

I was not only thinking about the good things Jesus has done for me.I was also thinking about the bad things that he did not take? As Christians we all battle the devil and his crew of misfits. Through the power, and might of our **Lord Jesus!!** We can win our day to day battles. Make no mistake my dear friend we are at war against a powerful enemy called the devil!

Eph. 6:11- Put on the whole armor of God, that ye may be able to stand against the Wiles of the devil.

6:12-for we wrestle not against flesh and blood, but against principalities, against powers, against the rulers of the darkness of this world, against spiritual wickedness in high places.

Praise God!! He gives us the ability to win our battles.

1 John.4:4- ye are of God, little children, and have overcome them: because greater is he that is in you,than he that is in the world.

Be encouraged friends!!! Although ***Jesus!!*** Leaves us some battles to fight; he has also given us the ability to win our battles, and become the warrior he has designed us to be.

"MY DAY ON CALVARY"

A year down the road I sit and look,
At the things Jesus left and the things Jesus took.
He took from me an eternity in hell.
Bestowed upon me the living well.
He took from me the sting of death.
Gives me life in every breath.
Gave unto me the desire to be kind.
Forgives me daily for my evil mind.
He took from me my sin and despair.
Blesses me fully with love and care.
A thousand pictures could never describe.
How it feels to no longer hide.
He picked me up when I was chained and bound.
And placed my feet on holy ground.
Most of all what he took from me.
Was my day to suffer on Calvary.
Tim Byrd 5.10.15

REBEL SOULS:

I was inspired to write this poem after participating in a bible study on the book "12 Ordinary Men" By John McArthur. **Bro. Tony Harmon.** Taught the study while I was at "the mission" Bro. Tony is one of many people who contribute their time to "The Mission" Bro. Tony is the music director at highland Baptist in Laurel, MS. Bro. Tony teaches a class at "The Mission" every Tuesday morning at 6:00 A.M. I was fortunate enough to get to know Bro. Tony, and his family During my stay at the mission.

The thought I want to develop is the fact the 12 disciples *Jesus!!* Chose were just "ordinary men" but *Jesus!!* Was able to mold the disciples into the vessels the holy spirit used to start the church and establish the Christian faith. This is the same process I am going through. I am being molded to preach the truth of *"GOD'S" Word* the way *"GOD"* wants me to.

Isaiah.64:8- But now, O Lord, thou art our father; we are the clay, and thou our potter; and we all are the work of thy hand.

The disciples went on to become the great apostles of the 1st century church, and they all could have been considered "**Rebels**" all of the Apostles suffered persecution, and all but one died horrific deaths at the hands of their persecutors.

1. Matthew: Suffered martyrdom in Ethiopia, killed by a sword wound.

2. Mark: Was not an apostle, but was one of the first missionaries.

Mark died in Alexandria, Egypt. After being dragged by horses through the streets until he was dead.

3. Luke: Not an apostle but was Paul's doctor. Luke was hanged in Greece as a result of his tremendous preaching to the lost.

4. John: Faced martyrdom when he was boiled in a huge basin of oil during a wave of persecution in Rome.

However; he was miraculously delivered from death. John was then sentenced to the mines on the prison island of Patmos. John wrote his prophetic book of "Revelation" while on Patmos. The apostle John was later freed and returned to serve as bishop of Edessa in modern Turkey.

John was the only Apostle to die peacefully as an old man.

5. Peter: Peter was crucified upside down on an X shaped cross. After seeing his wife crucified as well. According to church tradition Peter told his tormentors he felt unworthy to die in the same way Jesus Christ had died.

6. James: James was the leader of the church at Jerusalem.when James refused to deny his faith in Christ he was thrown over one hundred feet down from the southeast pinnacle of the temple. When his persecutors discovered James had survived the fall they beat him to death with a fullers club.

* This was the same pinnacle where Satan had taken ***Jesus!!*** During the temptation.

7. James the son of Zebadee:

Was a fisherman by trade when Jesus called him to a lifetime of ministry. James was a strong leader of the church, and was ultimately beheaded in Jerusalem. The Roman officer who guarded James watched in amazement as James defended his faith at his trial. Later at the execution of James the Roman guard proclaimed his new found faith in **Jesus!! Christ** knelt down with James to accept beheading as a Christian.

8. Bartholomew: Also known as **Nathaniel** was a missionary to Asia. He witnessed for our Lord in present day turkey. Bartholomew was martyred for his preaching in Armenia where he was flayed to death with a whip.

9. **Andrew:** Andrew was crucified on an X shaped cross in Patras Greece, after being severely whipped by seven soldiers. To prolong Andrew's agony the Soldiers tied Andrew to the cross with cords. Andrew's followers reported that as Andrew was led to the cross he saluted the cross and spoke these words."I have long desired and expected this happy hour. The cross has been consecrated by the body of Christ hanging on it." Andrew continued to preach the gospel to his crucifiers for two days until he expired.

10. Thomas: Thomas was stabbed with a spear in India during one of his missionary trips to establish the church in the sub-continent.

11. Jude: Jude was killed with arrows when he refused to deny his faith in Christ.

12. Mathias: Mathias was chosen to replace the traitor Judas Iscariot.

Mathias was stoned then beheaded.

13. Paul: Paul was known as Saul the persecutor of Christians before his conversion on the Damascus road.

Paul was tortured then beheaded by the evil emperor Nero at Rome in A.D 67. Paul endured a lengthy imprisonment which allowed him to write his many epistle's to the church's he had formed through out the Roman empire. These 13 epistle's teach many of the foundational doctrines of Christianity and form a large part of the new testament.

14. Simon the zealot: Simon was traditionally martyred by being sawn in half.

15. Phillip: Phillip evangelized in Phrygia. Hostile Jews had him tortured, and then crucified upside down. Some sources have him being stoned to death.

16. Stephen: was not an apostle but one of the first seven deacons appointed in the new testament church. Stephen was the first recorded martyr of the new testament church. Stephen was stoned to death outside the city wall of Jerusalem as a young Pharisee named Saul (who later became the apostle paul) looked on in approval. Stephens last recorded comments was. "I see the heavens opened up and the son of man standing on the right hand of God" and as he was dying he cried with a loud voice "Lord lay not this sin to their charge"

These 16 men I have listed was among the many martyrs of the 1st century church. However there has been more martyr's since the year 1900 than all of the martyr's since Christ.

"REBEL SOULS"

The bible tells us who Jesus chose.
He has a soft spot for rebel souls.
He chose a tax collector named Matthew.
Told saul the persecutor; "you will do"
He told Andrew and Peter at the sea of Gallilee.
To be fishers of men; "come follow me"
He was allways performing signs and wonders.
He chose two brother's named "the sons of thunder"
One was chosen who betrayed the son of man.
Sold out our Lord for merely silver in hand.
Taken from the garden, he continued to the cross.
He loved us enough to pay the ultimate cost.
He commissioned us all to go and tell the world.
Of a friend named Jesus; our Savior,our lord.
I stand in amazement,its still hard to believe.
He suffered the cross for a rebel like me.
Tim Byrd 1.3.16

I hope you have enjoyed reading this book it has been a great pleasure and a very educational task for me. Today is January 14th 2016 which is my youngest brother Sam's birthday and the birthday of my brother in Christ, and ministry partner Raju Amruthapudi as well, so its a great day to finish the book. It has taken me the better part of two years to reach this point, and I have pretty much said all I have felt led to say. I would like to say **Thank you** one last time to everyone who has helped me with this project. **Thank you!!** To all who have supported "Continuing Strength International Ministries" and our desire to do God's work in the country of India.

Closing prayer: Our most gracious heavenly Father, I come to you Father in the name of Jesus, I ask you Father to forgive me for my sins dear Lord. I'm still a sinner Father and I ask you to forgive me for my sins and hear my prayer Father. I love you Father and I praise your Holy Name Father. Thank you Father for sending Jesus to die for my sins and thank you Father for my salvation and the joy you provide, I ask you Father to use these words and this book to touch the hearts of the lost and the hurting Father. I've done what you have commissioned me to do Father and from here on out dear Lord this book and the fruit it yields is in your hands Father and I ask you to bless it as you see fit according to your will Father. Thank you for what your gonna do Father in the name of Jesus I pray. Amen.

www.ingramcontent.com/pod-product-compliance
Ingram Content Group UK Ltd.
Pitfield, Milton Keynes, MK11 3LW, UK
UKHW041944230426
12048UKWH00008B/123